Copyright © 1984 Lion Publishing

Published by
Lion Publishing plc
Icknield Way, Tring, Herts, England
ISBN 0 85648 857 7
Lion Publishing Corporation
10885 Textile Road, Belleville, Michigan 48111, USA
ISBN 0 85648 857 7
Albatross Books
PO Box 320, Sutherland, NSW 2232, Australia
ISBN 0 86760 579 0

First edition 1984

Acknowledgements
Copyright hymns: 'Tell out my soul' by
kind permission of Timothy Dudley-Smith
Scripture quotations: from the *Holy Bible,
New International Version*, copyright New York
International Bible Society, 1978
Photographs by Sonia Halliday Photographs as follows: F. H. C. Birch,
'Praise, my soul, the King of Heaven', 'Now thank we all our God',
'Amazing Grace', 'To God be the glory!', 'Abide with me', and cover;
Sister Daniel, 'All things bright and beautiful', 'We plough the fields',
'Rock of ages', 'When I survey the wondrous Cross', 'Love divine', 'The
Lord's my shepherd'; Sonia Halliday, 'Glorious things of thee are spoken',
'There is a green hill', 'Dear Lord and Father of mankind', 'Eternal Father,
strong to save', 'O come, all ye faithful', The day thou gavest', and
endpapers; Laura Lushington, 'Tell out, my soul, the greatness of the
Lord'; Jane Taylor, 'Guide me, O thou great Jehovah'; Barbara Warley,
'Once in royal David's city'

British Library Cataloguing in Publication Data

Idle, Christopher
  Hymns of praise.—New ed.
  1. Hymns, English
  I. Title   II. Idle, Christopher. Lion book
  of favourite hymns
  264'.2   BV459
  ISBN 0-85648-857-7

Printed and Bound in Great Britain by
Purnell and Sons (Book Production) Ltd.,
Paulton, Bristol

Hymns
of Praise

COMPILED BY CHRISTOPHER IDLE

A LION BOOK

Tring · Belleville · Sydney

PRAISE, MY SOUL,
THE KING OF HEAVEN

A tiny and remote country parish in Southern Ireland did not seem the ideal place for the brilliant young graduate to start his ministry — six feet tall with dark, curly hair, a classical scholar with great gifts as a speaker. But here in County Wexford, as a brash new curate, Henry Francis Lyte had an encounter which turned his ideas inside out.

A neighbouring clergyman was terminally ill. He confessed to Lyte that he had begun to re-examine his life as he read and studied the New Testament. He urged his younger friend to do what he had at last done: to stop relying on religious duties and good deeds for his peace with God, but trust completely in the mercy of Christ and his saving power.

This meeting immediately checked Lyte's contempt for the Methodists and 'enthusiasts' in the area. It gave him for the first time a truly personal faith. And it inspired him to write hymns such as this famous version of Psalm 103.

Praise, my soul, the King of heaven;
  To his feet thy tribute bring.
Ransomed, healed, restored,
    forgiven,
  Who like thee his praise should
    sing?
Praise him! Praise him!
Praise the everlasting King.

Praise him for his grace and favour
  To our fathers in distress;
Praise him still the same for ever,
  Slow to chide, and swift to bless.
Praise him! Praise him!
Glorious in his faithfulness.

Father-like, he tends and spares us;
  Well our feeble frame he knows;
In his hands he gently bears us,
  Rescues us from all our foes.
Praise him! Praise him!
Widely as his mercy flows.

Angels in the height, adore him;
  Ye behold him face to face;
Sun and moon, bow down before
    him;
  Dwellers all in time and space.
Praise him! Praise him!
Praise with us the God of grace.

HENRY FRANCIS LYTE (1793-1847)

TELL OUT, MY SOUL,
THE GREATNESS OF THE LORD

The seventeenth century was the great age of Bible translation. Parts of the eighteenth and nineteenth were boom periods for new hymns. The second half of the twentieth century has seen a flood of exciting new versions of the Bible in English as well as an upsurge of contemporary hymn-writing.

When Timothy Dudley-Smith was sent a review copy of the 1961 *New English Bible*, he was very struck by the beginning of Luke's Gospel. In this version, the *Magnificat*, or 'Song of Mary', begins with the words 'Tell out, my soul, the greatness of the Lord'. They inspired him to write this paraphrase, which is now one of the most popular of modern hymns. It is the only hymn in our book by a living author, but it stands as a reminder that the tradition of writing and singing new Christian songs is thriving today.

> Tell out, my soul, the greatness of the Lord!
> Unnumbered blessings, give my spirit voice;
> Tender to me the promise of his word;
> In God my Saviour shall my heart rejoice.
>
> Tell out, my soul, the greatness of his name!
> Make known his might, the deeds his arm has done;
> His mercy sure, from age to age the same;
> His holy name — the Lord, the Mighty One.
>
> Tell out, my soul, the greatness of his might!
> Powers and dominions lay their glory by.
> Proud hearts and stubborn wills are put to flight,
> The hungry fed, the humble lifted high.
>
> Tell out, my soul, the glories of his word!
> Firm is his promise, and his mercy sure.
> Tell out, my soul, the greatness of the Lord
> To children's children and for evermore!

TIMOTHY DUDLEY-SMITH (b. 1926)

GLORIOUS THINGS
OF THEE ARE SPOKEN

Today we usually expect a service in church to start with a hymn. But 200 years ago it was different — only the psalms could be sung.

John Newton played an important part in the battle to have hymns accepted in church. While in Liverpool, he and his wife Mary would often spend an hour on Sunday evenings praying and singing with friends. In his first parish as a minister, at Olney in Buckinghamshire, the week-night meeting where this hymn was first sung soon had to move to larger premises. And on Sundays, Newton's ministry attracted so many to the services that a gallery had to be built in the church to make room for everybody!

Glorious things of thee are spoken,
    Zion, city of our God;
He whose word cannot be broken
    Formed thee for his own abode.
On the Rock of ages founded,
    What can shake thy sure repose?
With salvation's walls surrounded,
    Thou may'st smile at all thy foes.

See! the streams of living waters,
    Springing from eternal love,
Well supply thy sons and daughters,
    And all fear of want remove.
Who can faint while such a river
    Ever flows their thirst to assuage?
Grace which, like the Lord the giver,
    Never fails from age to age.

Round each habitation hovering,
    See the cloud and fire appear
For a glory and a covering,
    Showing that the Lord is near.
Thus they march, the pillar leading,
    Light by night and shade by day;
Daily on the manna feeding
    Which he gives them when
        they pray.

Saviour, if of Zion's city
    I through grace a member am,
Let the world deride or pity,
    I will glory in thy name.
Fading is the worldling's pleasure,
    All his boasted pomp and show;
Solid joys and lasting treasure
    None but Zion's children know.

JOHN NEWTON (1725-1807)

ALL THINGS
BRIGHT AND BEAUTIFUL

The chief writer of hymns for children in the nineteenth century was undoubtedly Mrs Cecil Frances Alexander, whose husband became primate of all Ireland. She wanted to help children understand the Christian faith. Of her 400 hymns, several were written to explain the meaning of phrases from the Apostles' Creed. 'All things bright and beautiful' explains in language children can understand the Creed's opening words: 'I believe in God, the Father Almighty, Maker of heaven and earth.'

All things bright and beautiful,
All creatures great and small,
All things wise and wonderful,
The Lord God made them all.

Each little flower that opens,
  Each little bird that sings,
He made their glowing colours,
  He made their tiny wings.

The cold wind in the winter,
  The pleasant summer sun,
The ripe fruits in the garden,
  He made them every one.

The purple-headed mountain,
  The river running by,
The sunset, and the morning
  That brightens up the sky.

The tall trees in the greenwood,
  The meadows where we play,
The rushes by the water
  We gather every day:

He gave us eyes to see them,
  And lips that we might tell
How great is God Almighty
  Who has made all things well.

CECIL FRANCES ALEXANDER (1818-95)

NOW
THANK WE ALL OUR GOD

Germany in the seventeenth century was in the throes of the Thirty Years' War. Martin Rinkart was a Lutheran pastor in the walled city of Eilenberg in Saxony. In spite of his frail physique, he stayed there throughout the war, enduring the horrors of famine and plague. He helped refugees from other areas who came to the city. When all the other pastors had either fled or died, he ministered to the sick and dying, and conducted some 4,500 funerals, including that of his own wife. Towards the end of the war, the city was besieged or overrun, once by the Austrians and twice by the Swedes. The Swedish general demanded a vast levy from Eilenberg's already desperate citizens; Martin pleaded with him, but in vain. So he turned to his friends and said, 'Come, my children; we can find no mercy with man — let us take refuge with God.' The general was so moved at seeing pastor and people praying and singing on their knees that the demand was reduced to less than a twentieth of the original sum.

This hymn, which began as a family grace said before meals, was sung as a national thanksgiving at the end of the Thirty Years' War.

Now thank we all our God
  With hearts and hands and voices,
Who wondrous things hath done,
  In whom his world rejoices;
Who from our mother's arms
  Hath blessed us on our way
With countless gifts of love,
  And still is ours today.

O may this bounteous God
  Through all our life be near us,
With ever joyful hearts
  And blessèd peace to cheer us;
And keep us in his grace,
  And guide us when perplexed,
And free us from all ills
  In this world and the next.

All praise and thanks to God
  The Father now be given,
The Son, and Holy Ghost,
  Supreme in highest heaven;
The one eternal God,
  Whom earth and heaven adore
For thus it was, is now,
  And shall be evermore.

MARTIN RINKART (1586-1649)
translated by CATHERINE WINKWORTH (1827-78)

WE PLOUGH THE FIELDS

This hymn was written by a layman. The author of the original German words was in turn a Commissioner of Agriculture and Manufacture, a newspaper editor and a bank auditor. His Christian faith wavered under the influence of the eighteenth-century view that man was his own saviour and master of his own destiny. But after a serious illness he turned again to the Maker of all things, and the heavenly Father who loves and cares for his children.

He wrote this hymn as part of a dramatic sketch; its theme was the festival of harvest thanksgiving at a German farmhouse.

We plough the fields, and scatter
   The good seed on the land,
But it is fed and watered
   By God's almighty hand:
He sends the snow in winter,
   The warmth to swell the grain,
The breezes and the sunshine,
   And soft refreshing rain:
All good gifts around us
   Are sent from heaven above;
Then thank the Lord, O thank the Lord,
   For all his love.

He only is the maker
   Of all things near and far,
He paints the wayside flower,
   He lights the evening star.
The winds and waves obey him,
   By him the birds are fed;
Much more to us, his children,
   He gives our daily bread:

We thank thee, then, O Father,
   For all things bright and good,
The seed-time and the harvest,
   Our life, our health, our food:
Accept the gifts we offer
   For all thy love imparts,
And, what thou most desirest,
   Our humble, thankful hearts.

MATTHIAS CLAUDIUS (1740-1815)
translated by JANE M. CAMPBELL (1817-78)

THERE IS A GREEN HILL

Mrs Alexander was the daughter of a major and the wife of a bishop. She was a tireless visitor, going from cottage to cottage in all weathers, supporting her husband's work in his diocese in Northern Ireland.

This hymn, dating from before her marriage, was written at the bedside of a child who was ill. The profits from *Hymns for Little Children*, where it first appeared in print, went to a school for deaf and dumb children in Londonderry. And Mendelssohn's friend William Horsley, who wrote the famous tune, was organist for eighteen years at a home for orphan girls in London.

The girl for whom the words were written recovered from her illness, and always regarded the hymn as especially hers, even when she grew up. Its greatness lies in the fact that so many other adults have done the same.

There is a green hill far away
    Outside a city wall,
Where the dear Lord was crucified,
    Who died to save us all.

We may not know, we cannot tell,
    What pains he had to bear,
But we believe it was for us
    He hung and suffered there.

He died that we might be forgiven,
    He died to make us good,
That we might go at last to heaven,
    Saved by his precious blood.

There was no other good enough
    To pay the price of sin;
He only could unlock the gate
    Of heaven, and let us in.

O dearly, dearly has he loved,
    And we must love him too,
And trust in his redeeming blood,
    And try his works to do.

CECIL FRANCES ALEXANDER (1818-95)

ROCK OF AGES

It was August 1756. A small group of people was meeting in a wooden barn in a village in Southern Ireland. The speaker, a layman named Morris, could hardly spell his own name, but he could read and understand the apostle Paul's words in Ephesians: 'But now in Christ Jesus ye who sometimes were far off are made nigh by the blood of Christ.' And, as he spoke, sixteen-year-old Augustus Toplady put his trust in Christ for the first time.

Toplady's most famous hymn grew from a single four-line verse appearing in *The Gospel Magazine*. He could be a bitter and obsessive controversialist, but this hymn has outlasted all his volumes of argument.

Rock of ages, cleft for me,
Let me hide myself in thee.
Let the water and the blood
From thy riven side which flowed
Be of sin the double cure,
Cleanse me from its guilt and power.

Not the labours of my hands
Can fulfil thy law's demands;
Could my zeal no respite know,
Could my tears for ever flow,
All for sin could not atone;
Thou must save, and thou alone.

Nothing in my hand I bring;
Simply to thy cross I cling;
Naked, come to thee for dress,
Helpless, look to thee for grace;
Foul, I to the fountain fly:
Wash me, Saviour, or I die!

While I draw this fleeting breath,
When my eyelids close in death;
When I soar through tracts unknown,
See thee on thy judgement throne,
Rock of ages, cleft for me,
Let me hide myself in thee.

AUGUSTUS TOPLADY (1740-78)

WHEN I SURVEY
THE WONDROUS CROSS

Five-year-old Isaac Watts was asked by his father why he had giggled in the middle of their solemn family prayers. He said that through his fingers he had seen a mouse running up the bell-rope, and had suddenly thought,

'There was a mouse, for want of stairs,
Ran up a rope to say his prayers'!

But it wasn't until he was about twenty that he ventured to complain to his father about the grim verse of the metrical psalms they had to sing at Above Bar Chapel in Southampton. 'Try then whether you can yourself produce something better,' was the answer.

The young man who had learned Latin at four, Greek at nine, French at ten and Hebrew at thirteen, sat down to write straight away, and never looked back. In all, he wrote about 750 hymns. Many people regard this as the greatest of them all.

When I survey the wondrous cross
  On which the Prince of glory died,
My richest gain I count but loss,
  And pour contempt on all my
      pride.

Forbid it, Lord, that I should boast
  Save in the death of Christ my
      God;
All the vain things that charm me
    most,
  I sacrifice them to his blood.

See from his head, his hands, his feet,
  Sorrow and love flow mingled
    down!
Did e'er such love and sorrow meet,
  Or thorns compose so rich a
    crown?

His dying crimson like a robe,
  Spreads o'er his body on the tree;
Then am I dead to all the globe,
  And all the globe is dead to me.

Were the whole realm of nature
    mine,
  That were a present far too small;
Love so amazing, so divine,
  Demands my soul, my life, my all.

ISAAC WATTS (1674-1748)

AMAZING GRACE

A violent storm at sea was the turning-point in John Newton's life.

Motherless at six and sent to sea on his eleventh birthday, he soon became a teenage rebel. He was press-ganged into the navy and flogged for desertion. Newton became involved with the African slave-trade and came close to starvation while living in extreme poverty in Sierra Leone.

But in March 1748, at the age of twenty-three, he was on board a cargo ship which was fighting for its life against heavy seas and rough weather. Worn out with pumping and almost frozen, he called out for God's mercy at the height of the storm, and was amazed to be saved from almost certain death.

Newton's life had many twists and turns. Eventually he renounced his involvement with slave-trading and, at thirty-nine, became a minister in the church. He persuaded the young William Wilberforce to stay in politics, and joined him in the fight to abolish the slave-trade.

Amazing grace! how sweet the sound
That saved a wretch like me!
I once was lost, but now am found,
Was blind, but now I see.

'Twas grace that taught my heart to fear,
And grace my fears relieved;
How precious did that grace appear
The hour I first believed!

The Lord has promised good to me,
His word my hope secures;
He will my shield and portion be
As long as life endures.

Through many dangers, toils, and snares
I have already come;
'Tis grace that brought me safe thus far
And grace will lead me home.

Yes, when this heart and flesh shall fail
And mortal life shall cease
I shall possess within the veil
A life of joy and peace.

JOHN NEWTON (1725-1807)

TO GOD BE THE GLORY!

Fanny Crosby, the American singer and musician, was blind from the age of six weeks. She married her music teacher, Alexander Van Alstyne, who was also blind. She once signed an unusual contract with a publisher: to write three songs every week all through the year. In all she wrote many thousands.

Although American evangelists Moody and Sankey used this hymn on their missions, it did not become an immediate favourite. But Billy Graham featured it in his Harringay crusade in 1954 — and soon Londoners were singing it on their way home, in streets and bus queues and underground trains.

Dr Graham took it back to the United States, introduced it next at Nashville, Tennessee, and saw it take its place in the group of top favourites.

To God be the glory! great things he hath done!
So loved he the world that he gave us his Son.
Who yielded his life an atonement for sin,
And opened the life-gate that all may go in.

*Praise the Lord! Praise the Lord! Let the earth hear
    his voice!*
Praise the Lord! Praise the Lord! Let the people rejoice!
O come to the Father through Jesus the Son;
And give him the glory — great things he hath done!

O perfect redemption, the purchase of blood!
To every believer the promise of God;
The vilest offender who truly believes,
That moment from Jesus a pardon receives.

Great things he hath taught us, great things he hath done,
And great our rejoicing through Jesus the Son:
But purer and higher and greater will be
Our wonder, our transport, when Jesus we see!

FANNY CROSBY (1820-1915)

LOVE DIVINE

Court composer Henry Purcell and Poet
Laureate John Dryden were a powerful combination in late
seventeenth-century England. When they got together to
write a patriotic song — part of the opera *King Arthur* —
it was an ideal partnership:

> 'Fairest Isle, all isles excelling,
> Seat of pleasures and of loves,
> Venus here will choose her dwelling
> And forsake her Cyprian groves . . .

But for Charles Wesley, a generation later,
this was just not good enough. Venus, Jove and Cupid, he
felt, were getting more than enough honours paid to them;
so he wrote these new words to be sung to Purcell's tune.

Instead of pagan legends, Wesley's verses
are full of the Bible; instead of glorifying the mythical
deities of Mount Olympus, he wrote in praise of Jesus.

Love divine, all loves excelling,
  Joy of heaven, to earth come
    down!
Fix in us thy humble dwelling,
  All thy faithful mercies crown:
Jesu, thou art all compassion,
  Pure, unbounded love thou art:
Visit us with thy salvation,
  Enter every trembling heart.

Come, almighty to deliver,
  Let us all Thy grace receive;
Suddenly return, and never,
  Never more thy temples leave:
Thee we would be always blessing,
  Serve thee as thy hosts above,
Pray, and praise thee, without
    ceasing,
  Glory in thy perfect love.

Finish then thy new creation,
  Pure and spotless let us be;
Let us see thy great salvation,
  Perfectly restored in thee;
Changed from glory into glory,
  Till in heaven we take our place,
Till we cast our crowns before
    thee,
  Lost in wonder, love and praise!

CHARLES WESLEY (1707-88)

DEAR LORD
AND FATHER OF MANKIND

'I am really not a hymn writer', said the American poet who wrote these verses. And few who started to read *The Brewing of Soma* by John Greenleaf Whittier would guess what was coming. It is a long poem, describing at first how 'soma', an intoxicating drink, was made to prepare Indian worshippers for their frenzied Vedic rites. By way of contrast, at the end of the poem, Whittier turns to the God and Father of our Lord Jesus Christ.

Within twelve years of the poem's publication, these five verses were being used separately as a Christian hymn, and few now remember their origin. Whittier belonged to the Society of Friends, or Quakers, who, more than most Christian groups, have discovered the value of meditative silence in their worship of God.

Dear Lord and Father of mankind,
  Forgive our foolish ways!
Re-clothe us in our rightful mind,
In purer lives thy service find,
  In deeper reverence praise.

In simple trust like theirs who
    heard,
  Beside the Syrian sea,
The gracious calling of the Lord,
Let us, like them, without a word
  Rise up and follow thee.

O Sabbath rest by Galilee!
  O calm of hills above,
Where Jesus knelt to share with
    thee
The silence of eternity,
  Interpreted by love!

Drop thy still dews of quietness,
  Till all our strivings cease;
Take from our souls the strain and
    stress,
And let our ordered lives confess
  The beauty of thy peace.

Breathe through the heats of our
    desire
  Thy coolness and thy balm;
Let sense be dumb, let flesh retire;
Speak through the earthquake,
    wind, and fire,
  O still small voice of calm!

JOHN GREENLEAF WHITTIER (1807-92)

GUIDE ME,
O THOU GREAT JEHOVAH

It was a fiery open-air sermon
by Howell Harris, the Welsh evangelist, that
gave to young medical student William
Williams a new ambition and a new vocation.
And it was open-air preaching
that Williams himself took up after an abortive
start in the Church of England ministry. For
almost half a century he travelled over the
mountains, roads and tracks of Wales,
averaging some 3,000 miles a year on horseback
or on foot. Of the 800 hymns that he wrote in
Welsh, this is his greatest. The tune 'Cwm
Rhondda' did not appear until the twentieth
century, but it is now inseparable from the
words. And Welshmen are unrivalled singers of
it, not least in the open air.

Guide me, O thou great Jehovah,
  Pilgrim through this barren land;
I am weak, but thou art mighty,
  Hold me with thy powerful
    hand:
  Bread of heaven,
Feed me till I want no more.

Open now the crystal fountain,
  Whence the healing stream doth
    flow;
Let the fire and cloudy pillar
  Lead me all my journey through:
    Strong Deliverer,
Be thou still my strength and
    shield.

When I tread the verge of Jordan,
  Bid my anxious fears subside;
Death of death, and hell's
    destruction,
  Land me safe on Canaan's side:
    Songs of praises
I will ever give to thee.

WILLIAM WILLIAMS (1717-91)
translated by PETER WILLIAMS (1722-96) and others

THE LORD'S MY SHEPHERD

A voyage from Britain to India in 1830 was nearly a disaster. A ship was wrecked in a violent storm off the Cape of Good Hope. No lives were lost, but almost everything else was. Alexander Duff, educational statesman and the first missionary sent to India by the Presbyterian Church of Scotland, lost an entire personal library — all except two books: his Bible and a Scottish Psalm Book were washed ashore. He took that as a parable. From now on he would concentrate on essentials.

In India, his household began each day by singing a psalm. And the words of Psalm 23 came vividly to his mind as he saw a shepherd leading his sheep across a precipitous track in the northern mountains. The man carried a long rod, with a hook at one end to help the sheep, and an iron band at the other for beating off wild animals. The rod and the staff, said Duff, were both needed — for guidance and defence.

This Scottish version of the twenty-third psalm is the consistent favourite among metrical psalms sung today.

The Lord's my shepherd, I'll not want;
 He makes me down to lie
In pastures green; he leadeth me
 The quiet waters by.

My soul he doth restore again,
 And me to walk doth make
Within the paths of righteousness,
 E'en for his own name's sake.

Yea, though I walk in death's dark vale,
 Yet will I fear none ill,
For thou art with me, and thy rod
 And staff me comfort still.

My table thou hast furnishèd
 In presence of my foes;
My head with oil thou dost anoint
 And my cup overflows.

Goodness and mercy all my life
 Shall surely follow me;
And in God's house for evermore
 My dwelling-place shall be.

SCOTTISH PSALTER (1650)

ETERNAL FATHER,
STRONG TO SAVE

By 1950, the American writer Albert E. Bailey had made the Atlantic crossing by sea forty-nine times. And every Sunday on board, he says, this hymn was sung at the ship's morning service.

It is sung in war and peace, on great public occasions as well as by lifeboatmen or fishermen in lonely coastal villages — and now in many languages around the world too. It is only surprising that it was written by a landsman — a short, bespectacled schoolmaster whose health was never robust.

Eternal Father, strong to save,
Whose arm doth bind the restless wave,
Who bidd'st the mighty ocean deep
Its own appointed limits keep:
   O hear us when we cry to thee
   For those in peril on the sea.

O Christ, whose voice the waters heard
And hushed their raging at thy word,
Who walkedst on the foaming deep,
And calm amid the storm didst sleep:
   O hear us when we cry to thee
   For those in peril on the sea.

O Holy Spirit, who didst brood
Upon the waters dark and rude,
And bid their angry tumult cease,
And give, for wild confusion, peace:
   O hear us when we cry to thee
   For those in peril on the sea.

O Trinity of love and power,
Our brethren shield in danger's hour;
From rock and tempest, fire and foe,
Protect them wheresoe'er they go:
   Thus evermore shall rise to thee
   Glad hymns of praise from land and sea.

WILLIAM WHITING (1825-78)

ONCE, IN ROYAL DAVID'S CITY

For millions of radio listeners all over the world, Christmas begins with the clear treble voice of a Cambridge choirboy. Every year since 1919, this has been the opening hymn in the Service of Nine Lessons and Carols broadcast from King's College Chapel on Christmas Eve.

The hymn itself is much older than this particular service. It is one of the 1848 collection by Mrs Alexander, written to illustrate the words from the Apostles' Creed: '. . . born of the virgin Mary'.

Once in royal David's city,
  Stood a lowly cattle-shed,
Where a mother laid her baby
  In a manger for his bed.
Mary was that mother mild,
Jesus Christ her little child.

He came down to earth from
    heaven,
  Who is God and Lord of all;
And his shelter was a stable
  And his cradle was a stall.
With the poor and mean and lowly
Lived on earth our Saviour holy.

And through all his wondrous
    childhood
  He would honour and obey,
Love, and watch the lowly maiden
  In whose gentle arms he lay.
Christian children all must be
Mild, obedient, good as he.

For he is our childhood's pattern;
  Day by day like us he grew.
He was little, weak, and helpless;
  Tears and smiles like us he knew:
And he feeleth for our sadness
And he shareth in our gladness.

Not in that poor lowly stable
  With the oxen standing by
We shall see him, but in heaven,
  Set at God's right hand on high,
When like stars his children
    crowned
All in white shall wait around.

And our eyes at last shall see him,
  Through his own redeeming love;
For that child so dear and gentle
  Is our Lord in heaven above:
And he leads his children on
To the place where he is gone.

CECIL FRANCES ALEXANDER (1818-95)

O COME,
ALL YE FAITHFUL

Young William Ewart Gladstone, who later became British Prime Minister, greatly appreciated the services at Margaret Chapel in London's West End. For one thing, the sermons were short — never more than twenty minutes! More important, the congregation were 'the most devout and hearty that I have ever seen'.

The minister at that time was Frederick Oakeley — one of the leaders of the nineteenth-century Oxford Movement. He believed passionately in the power of ritual, religious symbols and fine music. And before he joined the Roman Catholic Church, he gave his congregation — and the world — this version of the eighteenth-century 'Adeste, fideles'.

O come, all ye faithful,
Joyful and triumphant,
O come ye, O come ye to Bethlehem;
Come and behold him,
Born the King of angels:
O come, let us adore him,
O come, let us adore him,
O come, let us adore him, Christ the Lord.

God of God,
Light of Light,
Lo! he abhors not the virgin's womb;
Very God,
Begotten not created:

Sing, choirs of angels,
Sing, in exultation,
Sing, all ye citizens of heaven above,
'Glory to God
In the highest':

Yea, Lord, we greet thee,
Born this happy morning,
Jesu, to thee be glory given!
Word of the Father,
Now in flesh appearing:

FREDERICK OAKELEY (1802-80)

ABIDE WITH ME

At the FA Cup Final at Wembley Stadium in April 1927, Cardiff City's 1-0 victory over Arsenal took football's oldest trophy out of England for the first and only time.

That match was also another 'first'. King George V was one of the 100,000 crowd who sang 'Abide with me' at a Wembley final for the first time. And since 1927 the hymn has always had a special link with Wembley. These words are now heard every Cup Final afternoon by a television audience of over 15 million in Britain alone, and by many more millions on radio and television around the world.

Abide with me; fast falls the eventide;
The darkness deepens; Lord, with me abide!
When other helpers fail, and comforts flee,
Help of the helpless, O abide with me.

Swift to its close ebbs out life's little day;
Earth's joys grow dim, its glories pass away;
Change and decay in all around I see;
O thou who changest not, abide with me.

I need thy presence every passing hour;
What but thy grace can foil the tempter's power?
Who like thyself my guide and stay can be?
Through cloud and sunshine, O abide with me.

I fear no foe with thee at hand to bless;
Ills have no weight, and tears no bitterness.
Where is death's sting? where, grave, thy victory?
I triumph still, if thou abide with me.

Hold thou thy cross before my closing eyes;
Shine through the gloom, and point me to the skies;
Heaven's morning breaks, and earth's vain shadows flee;
In life, in death, O Lord, abide with me!

HENRY FRANCIS LYTE (1793-1847)

THE DAY THOU GAVEST

By 1897 Queen Victoria had been Britain's sovereign for sixty years; no other English monarch had reigned so long. The Diamond Jubilee was celebrated in tens of thousands of churches — and centrally in London at Westminster Abbey. This hymn was specially chosen by the queen to be sung in every church on that occasion.

In the hymn-books it is usually found in the 'Evening' section; but John Ellerton wrote it, while a vicar in Crewe, for missionary meetings. Christians in the nineteenth century were becoming aware of their responsibility to take the gospel to the whole world, and this hymn clearly expresses their international vision. Even when Victoria's empire had crumbled away, the kingdom of Christ would remain.

The day thou gavest, Lord, is ended,
  The darkness falls at thy behest;
To thee our morning hymns ascended,
  Thy praise shall sanctify our rest.

We thank thee that thy Church unsleeping,
  While earth rolls onward into light,
Through all the world her watch is keeping,
  And rests not now by day or night.

As o'er each continent and island
  The dawn leads on another day,
The voice of prayer is never silent,
  Nor dies the strain of praise away.

The sun that bids us rest is waking
  Our brethren 'neath the western sky,
And hour by hour fresh lips are making
  Thy wondrous doings heard on high.

So be it, Lord; thy throne shall never,
  Like earth's proud empires, pass away;
Thy Kingdom stands, and grows for ever,
  Till all thy creatures own thy sway.

JOHN ELLERTON (1826-93)